KEEP GOING!

First published by Allen & Unwin in 2024

Allen & Unwin
Cammeraygal Country
83 Alexander Street
Crows Nest NSW 2065
Australia
Phone: (61 2) 8425 0100
Email: info@allenandunwin.com
Web: www.allenandunwin.com

Allen & Unwin acknowledges the Traditional Owners of the Country on which we live and work.
We pay our respects to all Aboriginal and Torres Strait Islander Elders, past and present.

 A catalogue record for this book is available from the National Library of Australia

ISBN (HB) 978 1 76118 015 6
ISBN (PB) 978 1 76118 099 6

For teaching resources, explore allenandunwin.com/learn

The illustrations in this book were created using a combination of traditional and digital techniques.

Cover and text design by Sandra Nobes
Set in 18 pt Akzidenz-Grotesk Pro Extended
This book was printed in September 2023 by C&C Offset Printing Co. Ltd, China

1 3 5 7 9 10 8 6 4 2

 MIX
Paper | Supporting responsible forestry
FSC® C008047

idanbb.com
chrisillo.com

Your BRAIN is a LUMP of GOO

Idan Ben-Barak

illustrated by
Christopher Nielsen

ALLEN&UNWIN
SYDNEY · MELBOURNE · AUCKLAND · LONDON

Hey. Hi.

I'm your brain.

You can't see me because I'm sitting

back here behind your eyes.

But I'll try to describe myself:

I'm about the **size** of a pineapple.

Like a pineapple, I have a hard outer cover.
It's called a **skull**.
I like it inside my skull.
It keeps me safe from getting bumped or squished
if you're not careful with me.

Fine

Hmmm

Hmmmmmm

Uh...

No

Nonononnonooooo!

I look like a lump of goo.

I feel soft, like jelly.

(Do NOT try to touch me.)

DO NOT
TOUCH

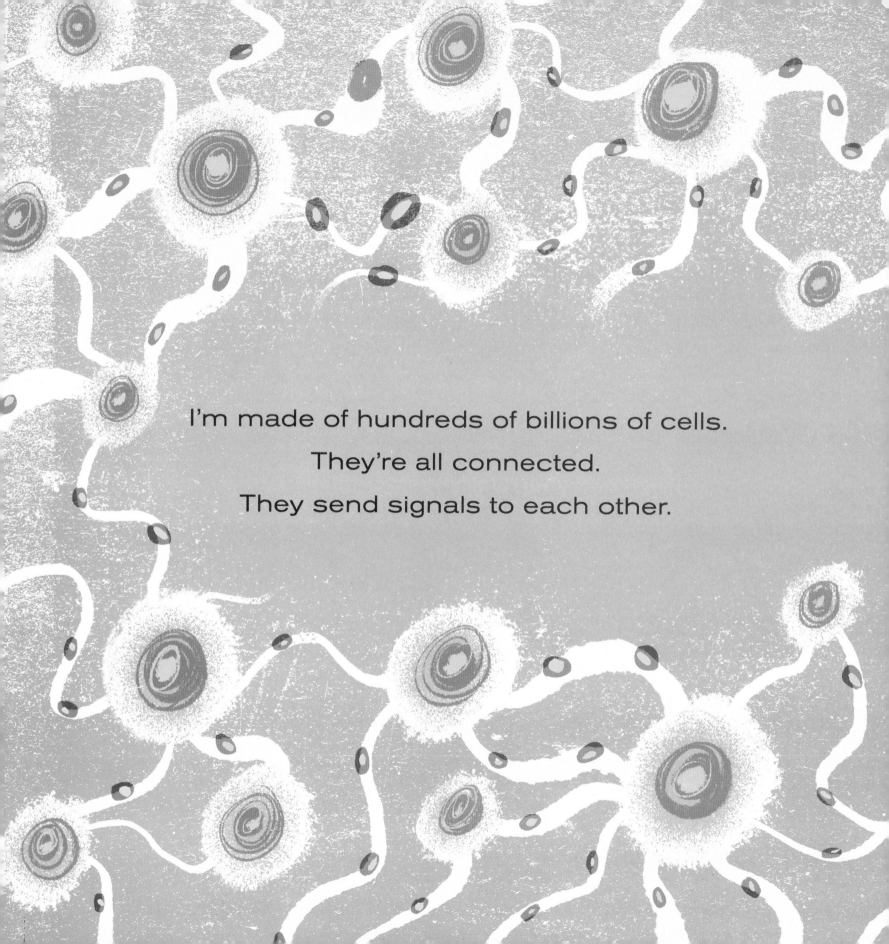

I'm made of hundreds of billions of cells.

They're all connected.

They send signals to each other.

Parts of me talk to other parts.

There's electricity running all over the place.

It's **very complicated**.

You don't notice any of that stuff, though.
It feels very different from within, doesn't it?

Nothing else in the world has that kind of 'within'.

I'm the part of you that is **YOU**.

Isn't that weird?

This is where it all happens.

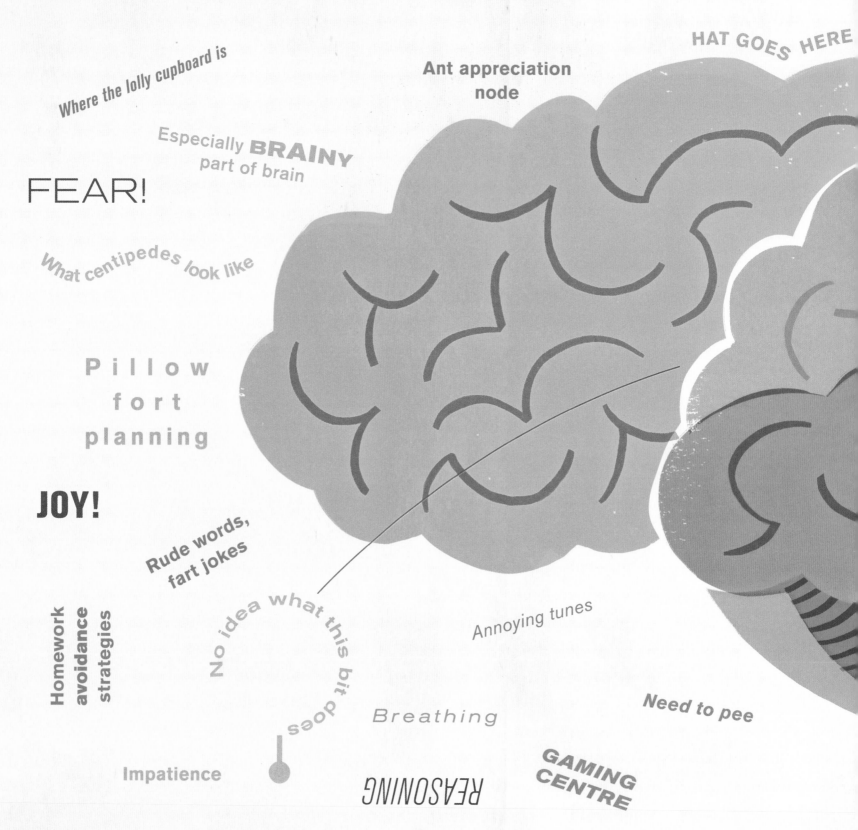

HAT GOES HERE

Ant appreciation node

Where the lolly cupboard is

Especially **BRAINY** part of brain

FEAR!

What centipedes look like

P i l l o w
f o r t
planning

JOY!

Rude words, fart jokes

No idea what this bit does

Homework avoidance strategies

Annoying tunes

Need to pee

Impatience

Breathing

REASONING

GAMING CENTRE

LEARNING

OUCH

EMOTIONS!

Daydreaming zone

Liking pizza

Not liking eggplant

How to JUMP

Dreaming

SLEEPING

Looking at things

Countdown to Christmas

YUCK

SIBLING annoyance CENTRE

HAPPINESS

Sneezing

GROWING

Funny faces

To the BODY →

To find out what the parts of the brain are called, turn to the end of the book. Not quite as far as the maze, though.

THOUGHTS!

I understand things.

I remember.

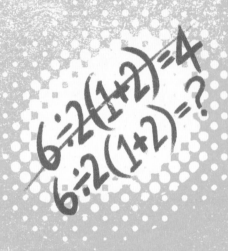

Except sometimes I forget.

Or I get **confused**, or **distracted**, or

overwhelmed.

I don't work very well
when I'm **tired**,
angry or **sad**.
Or too **excited**.

It's pretty easy to trick me.

Look, I'm **not** a computer.

Nobody planned me. Nobody built me.

It took me many millions of years to become what I am.

So I'm not perfect. I'm sorry.

But I **can** do lots of things by myself.
You don't need to pay attention
to how your body works.

I tell your lungs how to breathe.

I tell your legs how to walk.

I take care of it.

Sometimes I figure things out by myself.

Sometimes I make up tunes by myself.

It just happens.

At night, when we sleep, I imagine **weird things**.
Which pineapples don't do. Probably.

Like a pineapple, I started off small and grew over time.

But I keep **changing**.

By talking, by writing,

by drawing, by singing.

By thinking.

By imagining.

Which doesn't happen
with pineapples.

Us lumps of goo are very similar,
but there are differences.

We need all kinds of lumps
to make this world interesting.

Which is not the case with

pineapples.

We'd like to show you how the brain works. But we have two problems:

1. *No one really knows* how the brain works. There's still so much to learn.
2. What we *do* know is very hard to explain (and even harder to draw).

The brain's different parts are all connected and constantly exchange signals. Anything you do, such as reading a book or turning a page, involves several parts of your brain working together. It's always very busy in there, even if you don't always notice it. Also, the brain changes as we grow, and changes depending on how we use it.

But there is a kind of order to it all. Because our brain developed from our ancestors' smaller, simpler brains, we usually find the parts of the brain that *keep you alive* are near the base of the brain, closer to the body, and on the inside. The parts that *make you human* are mostly on the outside.

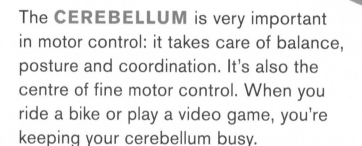

CAT BRAIN

The **CEREBELLUM** is very important in motor control: it takes care of balance, posture and coordination. It's also the centre of fine motor control. When you ride a bike or play a video game, you're keeping your cerebellum busy.

GOOSE BRAIN

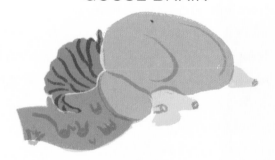

Here at the bottom is the **BRAIN STEM**. It leads signals from the body to the brain and back. It's also responsible for very basic, automatic and important tasks, like controlling your breathing, the beating of your heart, and digestion.

The **CEREBRUM** is the largest part of your brain. It's a lot smaller in other animals. The special thing about the human brain is that the cerebrum grew to be very big and now covers most of the rest of the brain, like a popcorn kernel that popped. We can divide the cerebrum into several areas, called 'lobes'. The **FRONTAL LOBE** controls movement; speech; problem-solving (thinking, reasoning, planning, making decisions); concentration; temper; personality; orientation. The **PARIETAL LOBE** gathers up a lot of information from your senses (like touch, pressure and pain) and integrates it with signals from other areas of the brain such as vision, hearing, motor, sensory and memory. The **TEMPORAL LOBE** is involved with hearing, understanding language, musical rhythm, visual memory, verbal memory and interpreting other people's emotions and reactions. The **OCCIPITAL LOBE**, at the back, has a lot to do with sight.

Oh, we should also mention that the cerebrum has two sides, right and left, so there are actually two of each lobe.

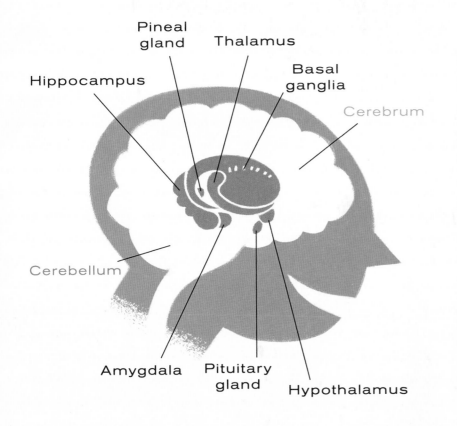

Pineal gland
Thalamus
Basal ganglia
Hippocampus
Cerebrum
Cerebellum
Amygdala
Pituitary gland
Hypothalamus

Deep inside your brain lie several very important parts. The **HYPOTHALAMUS** regulates your body temperature, hunger, thirst and (together with the **PINEAL GLAND**) sleep patterns. The **THALAMUS** controls attention and sorts out information from the rest of the brain. There's a lot happening in the **BASAL GANGLIA** that has to do with movement, emotions, habits and making decisions. The **HIPPOCAMPUS** is important for learning, dreaming, imagination, memory and navigation. The **AMYGDALA** is where we feel fear. The **PITUITARY GLAND** is responsible for growth and development of your body.

KEEP GOING!